BRANDO

BRANDO

IN THE CAMERA EYE

PHOTOGRAPHY AND COMMENTARY BY SAM SHAW

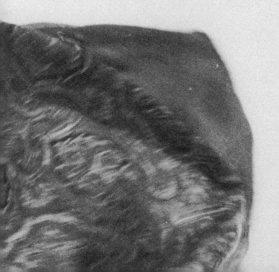

Exeter Books

NEW YORK

Copyright © 1979 by Peebles Press International, Inc.
An Exeter Book
Distributed by Bookthrift, Inc.
New York, New York
ISBN 0-89673-031-X

Entire project supervised by Sam Shaw

Design by Jacques Chazaud

Pictorial director: Marcus A. Cohen

Graphic Production by Filmar Graphics, Inc., San Diego, California

Photo Credits
Sam Shaw
Cover, title page, 6, 7, 9 - 123, 152, 153, back cover
UPI
124 - 151, 154 - 160

Hy Simon Archive: Omni Zoetrope
160

Printed and bound in the United States of America

CONTENTS

1

FOREWORD

I first met Marlon when he was on Broadway doing "A Streetcar Named Desire." Since then, I've shot him acting in a number of films. "Viva Zapata!" . . . "One-Eyed Jacks" (which he directed) . . . "The Fugitive Kind" . . .

My photographs and words in this book represent various creative moments in Brando's life, portraying him at work and at play.

As a professional photographer, it's been a terrific experience watching him before and behind the camera. All the crazy stories, the unexpected things people attribute to him, Marlon can top with wilder stories.

Brando denies turning acting into an art form. He derides acting, in fact. But he's made his whole life an art form.

I've always found him a truly committed, and highly unconventional individual.

Here then is what I've conceived as my candid tribute to one of the greatest actors of this age . . . and one of the most original and genuine men I know.

SAM SHAW

Brando does surprising things on the set . . . When you're taking pictures of him, you've got to be aware every moment, you can't relax, because he's going to do something exciting or something daffy suddenly . . .

Between scenes in "Viva Zapata!"

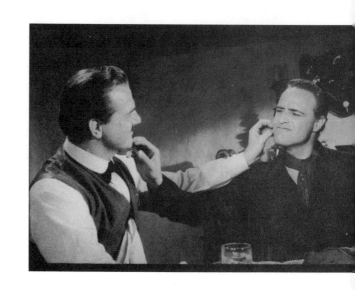

Karl Malden and Brando in a bit of horseplay on location for
"One-Eyed Jacks"

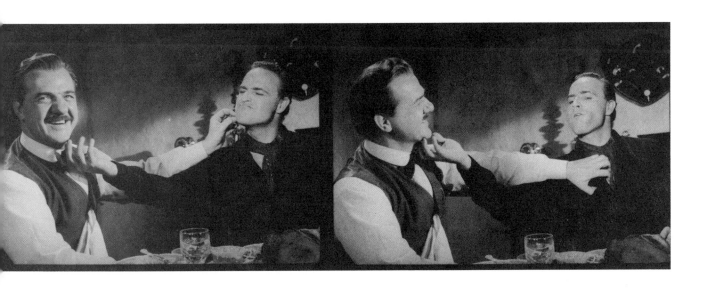

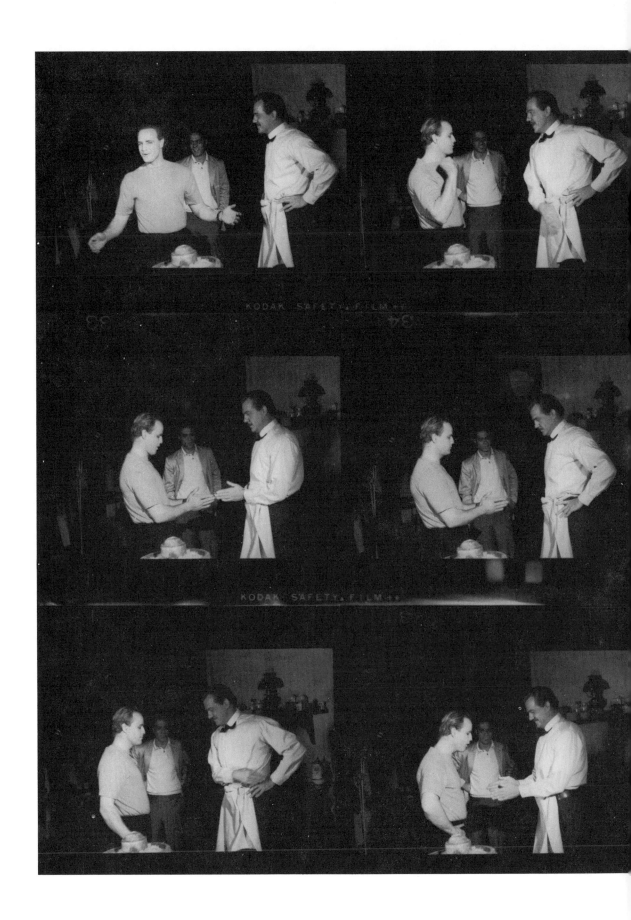

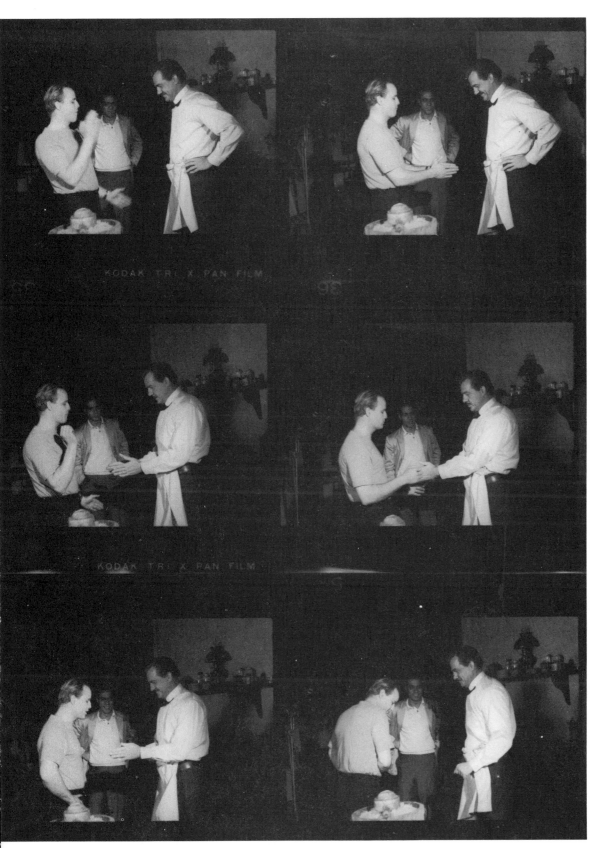

Karl Malden and Brando playing hand games for diversion during the filming of "One-Eyed Jacks"

In the middle of the most intense, serious scene he could also do something very humorous . . .

He makes funny faces . . .

He's a very human, very strange guy.

Elia Kazan told me that during the rehearsals for the stage production of "A Streetcar Named Desire," Brando would come over to his house and hang around.

He'd sit on the floor with Kazan's daughter and play high card, the simplest game, for three hours, four hours . . . Ace topping a king or three topping a two . . .

He's always been wonderful with kids.

Elia Kazan (l.) and his daughter (c., atop donkey) on location for "Viva Zapata!"

. . . a very human, very strange guy . . .

A very athletic guy . . . I think he could have been an Olympic athlete; he's one of the most athletic men I've ever come across.

He'd be standing still, and all of a sudden he'd high jump over a fence . . . 5½ feet over the thing, just like that — amazing!

I don't know, but some guys might qualify for events in amateur track meets on some of the things he did . . .

And in the middle of making a picture — playing football along the Pacific Coast. And he could throw . . .

And baseball . . . The baseball shot was taken at a picnic for the Actors Studio in Connecticut. Brando was very young; he was doing "Streetcar" on the stage at that time . . .